Thirty Days to a Better Marriage

By

Mark Sutton

RAGGED EDGE PRESS

This Ragged Edge Press publication
was printed by
Beidel Printing House, Inc.
63 West Burd Street
Shippensburg, PA 17257-0152 USA

In respect for the scholarship contained herein, the acid-free paper used in this book meets the guidelines for permanence and durability of the Committee on Production Guidelines for Book Longevity of the Council on Library Resources.

For a complete list of available publications
please write
Ragged Edge Press
Division of White Mane Publishing Company, Inc.
P.O. Box 152
Shippensburg, PA 17257-0152 USA

Library of Congress Cataloging-in-Publication Data

Sutton, Mark, 1947–
    Thirty days to a better marriage / by Mark Sutton.
        p.   cm.
    Includes bibliographical references.
    ISBN 1-57249-129-9 (alk. paper)
    1. Marriage.   2. Marriage--Religious aspects--Christianity.
3. Love--Religious aspects--Christianity.   4. Spouses--Religious
life. I. Title.
HQ734.S9775 1998
306.81--dc21   98-10077
                                                                    CIP

CONTENTS

INTRODUCTION

Is your marriage in trouble? Do you have difficulty communicating with one another? Is the "spark" gone?

If you answered "yes" to any of these questions, then I have some great news! *Thirty Days to a Better Marriage* was written just for <u>you</u>. And if you follow the suggestions in its pages for the next thirty days, I believe **your marriage will become stronger and healthier** than it's been in a long time.

This book has thirty chapters (or "days"), each of which can be read and completed in about fifteen minutes. Each "day" is divided into three sections: (1) a passage of scripture ("Preparing the Heart"); (2) a short devotional ("Changing the Heart"); (3) several exercises for both husband and wife ("Strengthening Exercises").

HOW TO GET THE MOST FROM THIS BOOK

- If at all possible, you and your spouse should read this book together.

- Decide on a time when the two of you can have fifteen minutes alone (that means without the children and <u>definitely</u> without the television).

- Try to take turns reading the different sections aloud.

- **The most important thing** you can do for one another is commit to staying with this book <u>for the entire thirty days.</u>

Remember, all you're asked to give up is **FIFTEEN MINUTES!!** Investing this small amount of time for one month can make your life—and your marriage—better than it's ever been.

Now, turn to Day One and begin transforming your marriage.

DAY ONE

PREPARING THE HEART

1 Corinthians 13:4–8a

4 Love is patient, love is kind. It does not envy, it does not boast, it is not proud. 5 It is not rude, it is not self-seeking, it is not easily angered, it keeps no record of wrongs. 6 Love does not delight in evil but rejoices with the truth. 7 It always protects, always trusts, always hopes, always perseveres. 8 Love never fails. (NIV)

CHANGING THE HEART

"Wait a minute!" I can hear you saying. "Love never fails? Paul must have been wrong when he wrote that!" You think immediately of your spouse, of failed dreams, of anger that simmers just beneath the surface of your relationship. And you come to the conclusion, "Love has not only failed in our marriage, it is *dead!*"

Eighteen years ago I heard similar words. Sitting in the living room of "Gene" and "Donna" (names have been changed), I watched a marriage in its final death throes.

Gene had just admitted having an affair with another woman. He no longer loved his wife. For her part, Donna had endured enough. She was ready for him to leave.

Bitter words were hurled by husband and wife. Both insisted there was nothing left to save; too much damage had been done.

The suitcases already packed and waiting by the front door gave mute testimony to the fact that the situation was desperate.

Silently I prayed for guidance. Then I began to talk, ask questions and, finally, make some suggestions.

The result? Gene and Donna stayed together. Though there were some rough times, their marriage grew in love and in trust. Today, eighteen years later, they are still man and wife. And they are more in love than ever.

God's Word is not wrong. Love does not have to fail.

In the coming days I will explain how your love can be renewed. I'll show you how your marriage *can* succeed. And I'll give you the same powerful helps that Gene and Donna received.

You see, it is <u>not</u> too late for your marriage.

STRENGTHENING EXERCISES

If the muscles in your body are to develop, they must be exercised. In the same way, we are going to exercise the weak parts of your marriage to make them stronger.

Be sure to do these exercises regularly.

Since this is the first session, we will begin with some easy exercises.

- Take your spouse's hand, look him/her in the eye and say, "I want my love for you to grow stronger and stronger."

- Promise one another you will read these devotionals <u>together</u> every night.

- Take a moment to pray together. Tell God you are willing for Him to make your marriage and your love for one another succeed.

DAY TWO

PREPARING THE HEART

Philippians 4:4–8

4 Rejoice in the Lord always. I will say it again: Rejoice! 5 Let your gentleness be evident to all. The Lord is near. 6 Do not be anxious about anything, but in everything, by prayer and petition, with thanksgiving, present your requests to God. 7 And the peace of God, which transcends all understanding, will guard your hearts and your minds in Christ Jesus. 8 Finally, brothers, whatever is true, whatever is noble, whatever is right, whatever is pure, whatever is lovely, whatever is admirable—**if anything is excellent or praiseworthy— think about such things.**

CHANGING THE HEART

Alfred got quite a shock. One morning he picked up the newspaper and read that he was dead! Somehow wrong information had been communicated. But after the shock wore off, Alfred began to get interested. After all, how often does anyone get to read his obituary?

As he scanned the world's record of his life, however, Alfred's heart sank. A wealthy man, he had made his fortune by inventing dynamite. The newspaper knew this and had dubbed him "the merchant of death."

Was this how he was going to be remembered, as a man who sold death? Alfred realized a change was in order. He wanted his life to count for good.

From that moment on Alfred Nobel worked for peace and harmony. Today the "merchant of death" is forgotten. But the Nobel Peace Prize is known around the world.

Learn a lesson from Alfred Nobel. No matter what kind of past your marriage has, it can still obtain a wonderful future. It all depends upon you.

And learn another lesson from the Bible. Don't major on the negatives in your marriage. Instead, look at what God wants to do for the two of you.

Alfred Nobel changed. And so can you.

STRENGTHENING EXERCISES

- Name three things you like about your marriage.

- Name three things you would like to see your marriage accomplish in the future.

- Tell your spouse one thing you like about him/her.

- Take a moment to pray together. Ask God to give your marriage a wonderful future.

DAY THREE

PREPARING THE HEART

1 Corinthians 12:12–18

12 The body is a unit, though it is made up of many parts; and though all its parts are many, they form one body. So it is with Christ. 13 For we were all baptized by one Spirit into one body—whether Jews or Greeks, slave or free—and we were all given the one Spirit to drink.

14 Now the body is not made up of one part but of many. 15 If the foot should say, "Because I am not a hand, I do not belong to the body," it would not for that reason cease to be part of the body. 16 And if the ear should say, "Because I am not an eye, I do not belong to the body," it would not for that reason cease to be part of the body. 17 If the whole body were an eye, where would the sense of hearing be? If the whole body were an ear, where would the sense of smell be? 18 But in fact God has arranged the parts in the body, every one of them, just as he wanted them to be.

1 Corinthians 12:26

If one part suffers, every part suffers with it; if one part is honored, every part rejoices with it.

CHANGING THE HEART

Have you ever noticed how different you are from your spouse? Unfortunately, those differences sometimes set us at odds with one another. Resentment begins creeping into the relationship as we realize our partner does not respond to the problems of life in the same way we do.

But <u>being different</u> is what we are all about!

Look at these facts:

- "Men and women *differ in every cell* of their bodies. This difference in the chromosome combination is the basic cause of development into maleness or femaleness...."[1]

- Women normally have a lower basal metabolism than men.

- The two sexes differ in skeletal structure. For example, the index finger on a woman's hand is normally <u>longer</u> than the ring finger. In a man, it is just the opposite. Women also normally have shorter legs, but a longer trunk.

- A woman's blood contains more water—and as a result, 20 percent fewer red cells.

- Women can stand high temperatures better than men can; and their metabolism slows down less.[2]

Yes, it's true! You and your spouse *really are different* from one another! And that's good news. You see, God tells us in this chapter that our differences can be used to create a **better, stronger marriage**.

The different parts of the body work together to sustain life in us. In the same way, our different talents must be forged into a common purpose—that of sustaining a loving relationship.

So...quit complaining that your spouse is not like you. God wants to use those differences to protect and strengthen both of you!

STRENGTHENING EXERCISES

- What are the differences that initially attracted you to your partner?

- How can the differences of your husband/wife be used to strengthen your marriage? Discuss this together.

- Take a moment to pray together. Thank God for the gifts He has given your spouse. Ask Him to help the two of you become stronger and more unified in your marriage.

DAY FOUR

PREPARING THE HEART

Ephesians 5:25–29

25 Husbands, love your wives, just as Christ loved the church and gave himself up for her 26 to make her holy, cleansing her by the washing with water through the word, 27 and to present her to himself as a radiant church, without stain or wrinkle or any other blemish, but holy and blameless. 28 In this same way, husbands ought to love their wives as their own bodies. He who loves his wife loves himself. 29 After all, no one ever hated his own body, but he feeds and cares for it, just as Christ does the church.

CHANGING THE HEART

Little Julie was explaining to her mother what she and her friends had been doing outside. "We played wedding! I was the bride, and Sarah was the bridesmaid. The baby girl from next door was the flower girl. It was a beautiful wedding!"

"That's very nice, dear," said the mother. "But who was the groom?"

With the confidence of a small child, Julie answered, "Oh, it was a small wedding—so we didn't have a groom!"

Men, let me ask you this: "Does your wife have a husband?"

Before you laugh off what seems to be a silly question, take a moment to look at <u>God's</u> definition of a husband. The above verses tell us:

- A husband loves his wife with the same love Christ has for us (vs.25).

- A husband gives of himself unselfishly in order to help his wife (vs.25).

- Everything he does is designed to help his partner become all she desires to be (vss.26–27).

- He loves his wife as much as he loves himself (vs.28).

- *He gives up his rights to better serve his wife* (vs.28).
"Does your wife have a husband?"

The question doesn't sound so silly now, does it? God has given you the model to follow. I challenge you to do the manly thing: become a godly husband.

Believe me, your wife will thank you for it.

STRENGTHENING EXERCISES

- Men, tell your wife 3 things you can do to become a better husband. List them on the next page under "Goals for Becoming a Godly Husband."

- Discuss together how you plan to accomplish these goals (keep this list; we will review it in the next several days).

- Now share with your wife how you want to become the best husband possible—a godly husband. Begin living for this purpose: to make your marriage as wonderful as God intended it.

GOALS FOR BECOMING A GODLY HUSBAND

_____

_____

_____

_____

_____

_____

_____

_____

_____

_____

_____

_____

_____

_____

_____

_____

DAY FIVE

PREPARING THE HEART

Ephesians 5:22–24

22 Wives, submit to your husbands as to the Lord. 23 For the husband is the head of the wife as Christ is the head of the church, his body, of which he is the Savior. 24 Now as the church submits to Christ, so also wives should submit to their husbands in everything.

Ephesians 5:33

33 However, each one of you also must love his wife as he loves himself, and the wife must respect her husband.

CHANGING THE HEART

A little boy had been fascinated one morning as his mother told him the story of how God took a rib from Adam and made Eve. Later that afternoon he was playing outside and got a pain in his side from running. As he doubled over he groaned, "Mom, I think I'm going to have a wife!"[3]

Let's face it. Marriage is painful for many people. So what can you, as a wife, do to make yours better?

God's Word gives you a powerful aid in verse 33. It says, "Respect your husband."

You may be shaking your head at this moment and saying, "It's obvious you don't know my husband!" You're right. But God knows your husband—and your Heavenly Father is the One who commands that you give your husband respect. The clue to accomplishing this is found in the spiritual analogy Paul uses in these verses. He is talking about Christ's love for us, the church.

How can Christ possibly love us? He sees us not only for what we are, He also sees us for <u>what we can be</u>.

Follow Christ's example. Respect your husband for <u>what he can be</u>.

Let these thoughts help you:

- God is not yet finished molding your husband.

- By respecting your husband, you encourage him to become all God wants him to be.

- In letting him become the spiritual head of the household, you free him to become a better Christian.

STRENGTHENING EXERCISES

- Women, tell your husband 3 things you can do to become a better wife. List them on the next page under "Goals for Becoming a Godly Wife."

- Discuss together how you plan to accomplish these goals (keep the list; we will review it in a few days).

- Women, tell your husband that you want to become the best wife possible—a godly wife. Begin living for this purpose: to make your marriage as wonderful as God intended it.

GOALS FOR BECOMING A GODLY WIFE

_____

_____

_____

_____

_____

_____

_____

_____

_____

_____

_____

_____

_____

_____

_____

_____

_____

DAY SIX

PREPARING THE HEART

Ephesians 5:31

31 "For this reason a man will leave his father and mother and be united to his wife, and the two will become one flesh."

Ephesians 5:33

However, each one of you also must love his wife as he loves himself, and the wife must respect her husband.

CHANGING THE HEART

Take a moment to look at your wedding band. Why do you wear it? And why on that particular hand and finger?

It is said that the custom of the wedding band began with ancient Greek civilization. According to their understanding of anatomy, the third finger on the left hand was connected by a special vein to the heart. By placing your spouse's band on that finger, you were *binding your heart to your partner.*[4]

Look again at verse 31. God says this bond with your spouse is so uniting that in His eyes you are one flesh.

Some of you reading this are very unhappy. Perhaps it is because you have been treating your partner—who is a part of yourself—shabbily, unfairly. Just as you cannot cut your arm without feeling it in your whole body, you cannot hurt your spouse without hurting yourself.

Remember, when God gave you the above verses, He did it for your protection. He loves you and wants you to have the best marriage and the best life possible.

One of God's rules for a happy marriage is this:

- The better you treat your spouse, the happier you become. For as you minister to your spouse, you are ministering to yourself.

Start following God's instructions for a good life today.

STRENGTHENING EXERCISES

- Look your spouse in the eye and express your love for him/her in words like this: "You are my partner for life. I love you. And I have decided to love you always."

- Make a list of three ways you have treated your spouse badly during this last year.

- Share the list with one another. Ask forgiveness for each action.

- Discuss how the two of you can begin to treat one another better. Write down the solutions on the next page under "Our Solutions to Problems." You will look at them again next week to see how you are progressing.

OUR SOLUTIONS TO PROBLEMS

_____

_____

_____

_____

_____

_____

_____

_____

_____

_____

_____

_____

_____

_____

_____

_____

DAY SEVEN

PREPARING THE HEART

Philippians 2:1–11

1 If you have any encouragement from being united with Christ, if any comfort from his love, if any fellowship with the Spirit, if any tenderness and compassion, 2 then make my joy complete by being like-minded, having the same love, being one in spirit and purpose. 3 Do nothing out of selfish ambition or vain conceit, but in humility consider others better than yourselves. 4 Each of you should look not only to your own interests, but also to the interests of others. 5 Your attitude should be the same as that of Christ Jesus: 6 Who, being in very nature God, did not consider equality with God something to be grasped, 7 but made himself nothing, taking the very nature of a servant, being made in human likeness. 8 And being found in appearance as a man, he humbled himself and became obedient to death—even death on a cross!

9 Therefore God exalted him to the highest place and gave him the name that is above every name, 10 that at the name of Jesus every knee should bow, in heaven and on earth and under the earth, 11 and every tongue confess that Jesus Christ is Lord, to the glory of God the Father.

CHANGING THE HEART

How can this passage on the sacrifice of Christ help your marriage? Pay special attention to verse five. Note again how God says our relationship with one another is to be patterned after Jesus Christ. With that in mind, let's look at two things which can help your marriage. The first is:

Equality

It's the word all the world seems to be using. Every racial group desires it. Both sexes fight for it. And if you're honest, you might admit that it has become a major source of conflict in your relationship.

God's Word has something very interesting to say about equality. **<u>GIVE IT UP!!!</u>**

Too radical, you say? Completely unrealistic? Worried you'll get trampled by your spouse?

God gives us these instructions to help us become **fulfilled**, not **frustrated**.

Remember Christ's attitude. Being God, He was equal with God. But He laid that equality aside to accomplish something wonderful: the redemption of mankind. And God the Father blessed Him for it.

So...what is **your** attitude? God has already said you are equal to your partner when it comes to His love.[5]

Let me encourage you to quit worrying about whether you receive equal things and equal privileges. Your marriage will be the stronger for it.

This change of attitude leads naturally to the second characteristic of a good marriage:

You must not do anything because of selfish ambition

What does this mean in the context of a marriage? It means
—any activity you engage in
—any attitude you hold
—any habit you have
—any person you insist on having as a friend
...ANYTHING that sacrifices the relationship you have with your spouse needs to be *seriously reevaluated*.

- In other words....**Think more of your spouse than you do of yourself**.

Remember, Christ redeemed mankind. In putting aside your worry about equality and control, you just might redeem your marriage...and make yourself happier in the process.

STRENGTHENING EXERCISES

- Ask your spouse to share with you three things he/she would truly like to do or have.

- What can you do <u>right now</u> to begin meeting the wishes on this list?

- What are you going to do <u>tomorrow</u> to continue meeting the wishes on this list?

- Come to an agreement on the solutions; write down both wishes and solutions on the next page under "Our Wish List." Sign and date the list. We will review it later.

- What one thing are you willing to give up to improve your marriage? Write it down on the "Our Wish List" as well.

OUR WISH LIST

_____

_____

_____

_____

_____

_____

_____

_____

_____

_____

_____

_____

_____

_____

_____

_____

_____

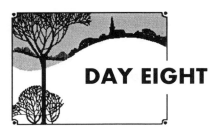

DAY EIGHT

PREPARING THE HEART

Song of Songs 8:6–7

6 Place me like a seal over your heart, like a seal on your arm; for love is as strong as death...It burns like blazing fire, like a mighty flame.

7 Many waters cannot quench love; rivers cannot wash it away. If one were to give all the wealth of his house for love, it would be utterly scorned.

CHANGING THE HEART

In a certain fairy tale, a huge troll asks a riddle of a boy named John. If he cannot correctly answer the riddle, the boy will forfeit his life.

The monster asks, "What is the strongest bond in the world?" John thinks for a moment, then responds haltingly, "One of my brothers is a sailor. He would probably say the strongest bond in the world is the horizon, for it joins the sky and sea together."

A troubled look crosses the boy's face. "But I have another brother who is a farmer. He would say the strongest bond in the world is the rainbow, for it joins the sun and rain together, making the crops grow."

Then the boy's face grows bright as a thought comes to mind. "But I think the strongest bond in the world is *love*! Because not even death can destroy it."[6]

The boy was right.

God's Word is very clear when it comes to the subject of Love. It is the most precious commodity in the world. Here we see the greatest love song in the world (The Song of Songs) saying that <u>anything</u> we trade for the love of our partner is to be despised.

So, be honest. Are you giving up a valuable gift from God to receive something far less precious? Or, to put it another way—have you taken something into your life that is destroying your marriage?

If you're not sure, ask your spouse. He or she will be able to tell you **immediately.**

Please listen carefully. And choose carefully. The success of your marriage depends upon how you answer the riddle.

STRENGTHENING EXERCISES

- Ask your spouse if you are giving up your love for something else.

- Do you agree? If not, why?

- What can you do to make your spouse feel better about your relationship?

- Together, decide how you can make your marriage stronger.

- Are both of you willing to give up whatever is necessary to keep your love forever?

- Review your "Goals for Becoming a Godly Husband" list.

DAY NINE

PREPARING THE HEART

James 1:2–4

2 Consider it pure joy, my brothers, whenever you face trials of many kinds, 3 because you know that the testing of your faith develops perseverance. 4 Perseverance must finish its work so that you may be mature and complete, not lacking anything.

1 Peter 1:6–7

6 In this you greatly rejoice, though now for a little while you may have had to suffer grief in all kinds of trials. 7 These have come so that your faith—of greater worth than gold, which perishes even though refined by fire—may be proved genuine and may result in praise, glory and honor when Jesus Christ is revealed.

CHANGING THE HEART

I'll go ahead and warn you ahead of time. You are **not** going to want to read this! But please stay with me. This devotional just might change your life and your marriage.

One afternoon in the highlands of Scotland, some men were gathered in a small pub comparing fish stories. One man, big and burly, was particularly animated in his tale of "the one that got away." As he tried to describe the size of the fish, his arm swung out and hit a waitress passing by. She, in turn, lost her grip on a glass of ale. It hurtled against a nearby wall and shattered. The brown stain spread quickly on the white surface, and no amount of wiping would erase it.

The wall, it seemed, was ruined.

While everyone was moaning about the situation, however, a man rose from another table to examine the wall. He then took a crayon from his pocket and, unnoticed, began to sketch. Under his hand a magnificent stag with spreading antlers soon began to emerge from the stain. And that which had been a terrible mistake became a thing of beauty.

The man was Sir Edwin Landseer. A master artist, he was known as England's foremost painter of animals.[7]

Have you ever thought about thanking God for the troubles in your marriage? If you haven't, go back and read the first scripture passage for today. James says we are to count it "pure joy" when we encounter difficulties in life! And the passage from 1st Peter says essentially the same thing.

Why would they say this?

God has created us so that we grow through experiencing trials and problems. Listen to what Charles Paul Conn says:

God created man something on the order of a rubber band. A rubber band is made to stretch. When it is not being stretched, it is small and relaxed, but as long as it remains in that shape, it is not doing what it was made to do. When it stretches, it is enlarged; it becomes tense and dynamic, and it does what it was made to do. God created you to stretch.[8]

Yes, do everything in your power to improve your marriage. But in the present, also ask God what **you** can learn from any problems your marriage has. It will not only make you happier and more at ease with your situation, you will also grow closer to God in the process.

Let the Master begin turning your problems into things of beauty.

STRENGTHENING EXERCISES

- Take a moment to privately talk to God. Tell Him about the major problems in your life.

- Ask God to give you a positive attitude about those problems.

- Ask Him to help you grow spiritually because of them.

- Begin looking for a way to turn your problems into assets.

- Review your "Goals for Becoming a Godly Wife" list.

DAY TEN

PREPARING THE HEART

Ephesians 5:1–2

1 Be imitators of God, therefore, as dearly loved children 2 and live a life of love, just as Christ loved us and gave himself up for us as a fragrant offering and sacrifice to God.

CHANGING THE HEART

There it is again: "Be imitators of God." Our Heavenly Father certainly has high standards for us! These verses tell us we should:

- Live a life of love;

- Love as Christ loves.

In order to understand how Christ lived and loved, we need to explore a concept that has lately fallen into disrepute.

Sacrifice. The world thinks of it as an ugly word. But God keeps gently pushing us to sacrifice in our lives and marriages.

David McKechnie makes this observation:

Mark it down. Anytime you see a happy family, it did not happen by accident. Somebody sacrificed. That person sacrificed convenience, comfort, time, power, and the right to make unilateral decisions. **There is no success without sacrifice.** *

We live in the era of the pampered athlete, executive, politician, educator, student, parishioner, preacher, and nation. What has happened to sacrifice? Sacrifice is the sacrament of love.[9]

"Sacrifice is the sacrament of love." What a powerful statement! It's how God proved His love for us. And like it or not, it's how you prove your love for God and for your spouse.

Give yourself a little test: by your actions and attitudes, does your spouse see a sacrificial love? Or does he/she see a shallow, selfish love?

Remember, you really don't have a choice if you are to follow God's Word.

Imitate God in your life. And begin <u>now</u>!

STRENGTHENING EXERCISES

- Ask your spouse to name one thing you do that he/she thinks is selfish on your part.

- Do you agree?

- Ask your spouse to help you moderate that particular behavior pattern or action.

- As you give up this behavior, realize that you are beginning to fulfill God's Word and imitate Christ's life.

* (My emphasis)

DAY ELEVEN

PREPARING THE HEART

Matthew 19:3–6

3 Some Pharisees came to him to test him. They asked, "Is it lawful for a man to divorce his wife for any and every reason?"

4 "Haven't you read," he replied, "that at the beginning the Creator 'made them male and female,' 5 and said, 'For this reason a man will leave his father and mother and be united to his wife, and the two will become one flesh' ? 6 So they are no longer two, but one. Therefore what God has joined together, let man not separate."

CHANGING THE HEART

Small, seemingly insignificant items are easily overlooked—but they can play a pivotal role in life. For example, look at one of the most important battles ever fought in the history of the world.

The year was 1066. On that date William, Duke of Normandy, invaded England. And he did it despite overwhelming odds.

The English had one of the most formidable fighting forces of that era, but William was confident his army could overcome them on the field of battle.

Why? Because of the **stirrup**.

The English did not yet know of this invention. They rode into combat in the same way they always had, then dismounted and fought on foot. With no support for their feet, they felt the horse was too unstable a platform from which to do battle. But the soldiers from Normandy were able to use the stirrups for support. They rode down the British soldiers as their horses advanced. From a higher position, it was easy to thrust home with their lances.[10]

Thus was history changed by a small invention.

Let me share with you another small item that can become a forceful weapon for fighting problems in your marriage. Overlooked by the world, it is nevertheless something every successful marriage must have. The object is actually a group of words put together to form two sentences. They go like this:

"I will **never** divorce you.   I choose to love you **always**."

When you say this, two powerful qualities begin to work in your marriage:

- You free your imagination from negative thinking about your marriage.

- You free your spouse to fully love you.

How does this help your marriage?

None of us wants to get hurt. If you threaten divorce during arguments, your spouse will begin erecting a protective shell to guard against the pain of your leaving. And that shell further separates you.

When you promise to stay through thick and thin, good and bad, everything changes. Your partner is then free to take down the shell and **surrender to the vulnerability of total love for you**.

I know it's risky to say these phrases. It's also risky to die on a cross for someone who doesn't even love you yet. But aren't you glad Christ took that risk!

Love as Christ loved. Take a step of faith today—for yourself and for your marriage.

STRENGTHENING EXERCISES

- Take your spouse's hand. Look him/her in the eye and say, "I will never again threaten divorce. I commit to loving you always."

- Share one thing you appreciate about your spouse.

- Together, ask God to bless your marriage—beginning today.

- Review the list "Our Solutions to Problems."

DAY TWELVE

PREPARING THE HEART

Proverbs 3:13–17

13 Blessed is the man who finds wisdom,
the man who gains understanding,
14 for she is more profitable than silver
and yields better returns than gold.
15 She is more precious than rubies;
nothing you desire can compare with her.
16 Long life is in her right hand;
in her left hand are riches and honor.
17 Her ways are pleasant ways,
and all her paths are peace.

CHANGING THE HEART

Wisdom and peace. How and where do you find them?

Once upon a time (goes this fairy tale for married couples) there was a man who had grown weary of his marriage and family. He wanted to find happiness; he wanted peace. The only thing to do, he decided, was to leave his wife and search for **The Magical City**. For in this wonderful place, he had heard, life was full, meaningful, rewarding.

So he left.

After several days of traveling, he found himself in a forest. "It would be easy to become lost in such a place," he said to himself. "Clever plans are called for." So before going to bed, he carefully took off his shoes and pointed them in the new direction he was going. Pleased with himself, he went to sleep.

But that night, while he slept, a jokester came along and *turned the man's shoes around*, pointing them in the opposite direction! Upon awakening the next morning, the traveler stepped into his shoes and continued on his journey.

After a few days he came to what he thought must be **The Magical City**. It was not as large as he had imagined it to be. And as he walked through its streets, it seemed as if he had been there before.

Soon he found a familiar street, knocked on the door of a familiar house, met a familiar family...and in his "Magical City" he lived happily ever after.[11]

For you, it's no fairy tale. Your "Magical City" is right where you live. Begin enjoying it today.

STRENGTHENING EXERCISES

- Take a moment to thank God for your home and family.

- What can you do <u>together</u> to make your home a happier place?

- Share this with your spouse.

- Review "Our Wish List."

DAY THIRTEEN

PREPARING THE HEART

1 Corinthians 7:2–5

2 But since there is so much immorality, each man should have his own wife, and each woman her own husband. 3 The husband should fulfill his marital duty to his wife, and likewise the wife to her husband. 4 The wife's body does not belong to her alone but also to her husband. In the same way, the husband's body does not belong to him alone but also to his wife. 5 Do not deprive each other except by mutual consent and for a time, so that you may devote yourselves to prayer. Then come together again so that Satan will not tempt you because of your lack of self-control.

CHANGING THE HEART

It was a special time. The husband and wife took a train to the small town where they'd spent their honeymoon thirty years earlier. For most of the afternoon they simply walked through the winding streets, sharing memories of that wonderful day. At one point the husband happened to look at his watch and gave a startled gasp. "Honey," he said, "we have less than ten minutes to get to the station and catch the return train!"

He began to run, but his wife just couldn't keep up. They arrived in time to see the last train of the day pulling out. Disgusted, the husband said, "I guess we'll just have to spend the night here."

As luck would have it, they stayed in the very room where their honeymoon began. Romantic thoughts filled the mind of the wife.

That night as they were preparing for bed, she looked at herself in the mirror. Thinking of the gray in her hair, she said softly, "Look honey. I have winter in my hair, but there's spring in my heart."

The husband responded, "Yeah, and if you hadn't had lead in your pants, we wouldn't have missed that train!"

Ah, romance! Why do so many marriages have problems in this area? It seems that when one partner is ready for romance, the other is not. Is it possible to make both husband and wife happy? The answer is a profound...**YES!**

In fact, I have some good news for your marriage. If you will follow the principles I give you in the next few days, I guarantee your love life will improve—in most cases, dramatically.

STRENGTHENING EXERCISES

- Not many exercises for this session. But they are important! They prepare you for the following days.

- Review the list "Our Solutions to Problems."

- Take your spouse's hand. Together, pray this prayer: "Dear Heavenly Father, we want our marriage to be stronger and more loving than it is right now. As we have placed our hands in each other's, please place your Hand of Blessing upon our marriage. We thank you for hearing and answering our prayer. In Jesus' Name, Amen."

- In the coming days you will be asked to pray at the end of almost every devotional. If one or the other of you is not comfortable praying, return to this prayer and use it.

DAY FOURTEEN

PREPARING THE HEART

1 Corinthians 7:4–5

4 The wife's body does not belong to her alone but also to her husband. In the same way, the husband's body does not belong to him alone but also to his wife. 5 Do not deprive each other except by mutual consent and for a time, so that you may devote yourselves to prayer. Then come together again so that Satan will not tempt you because of your lack of self-control.

CHANGING THE HEART

"I feel so used."

The couple sat in my office, not daring to look at one another. There was almost no romance in the marriage, almost no sex. The wife had just spat out the words beginning this devotional. Her anger was a response to the husband's saying, "My wife is frigid. We hardly ever make love anymore."

"I feel so used."

Since that day I've heard many other women say the same thing. And I've heard just as many husbands complain about a lack of physical love.

Who is right? Both? Neither?

Perhaps both are. Certainly the women whose husbands ignore them during the day, then climb into bed at night and expect instant love, have reason to imagine they are being used.

Sex, in today's world, has been separated from love. And the world is the poorer for it. Believe me when I say that the two go hand in hand. Men, I can even promise that if you put sex above love in your marriage, then the relationship between you and your wife is not very good.

Your wife needs to know that you love <u>her</u>. She wants to be assured that you don't just love her body, but that you love <u>her</u>.

"I feel so used."

The woman who said that in my office several years ago is to-day happily married to the same man. She and her husband's sexual relationship is better, according to them, than it has been in years.

The key? What I've just shared with you. And the tip I'll give you men tomorrow.

STRENGTHENING EXERCISES

- Share with each other one thing you enjoy about your love life.

- Suggest one thing you wish your spouse would do that could help your love life.

- Spend the next five minutes simply holding hands and talking about the good times in your marriage.

DAY FIFTEEN

PREPARING THE HEART

1 Corinthians 7:3

3 The husband should fulfill his marital duty to his wife, and like-wise the wife to her husband.

Song of Songs 4:10–12

10 How delightful is your love, my sister, my bride!
    How much more pleasing is your love than wine,
    and the fragrance of your perfume than any spice!
11 Your lips drop sweetness as the honeycomb, my bride;
    milk and honey are under your tongue.
    The fragrance of your garments is like that of Lebanon.
12 You are a garden locked up, my sister, my bride;
    you are a spring enclosed, a sealed fountain.

CHANGING THE HEART

Yesterday I promised you men a great tip that will improve your love life. Lest you think this is merely hyperbole, let me explain why I say it's a great tip. *Almost without exception, the couples who have come to me for counseling and who have followed this tip have dramatically improved the sexual and romantic part of their marriage.*

Here's the great tip:

IF YOU WANT LOVE <u>IN</u> THE BEDROOM, COURT YOUR WIFE <u>OUTSIDE</u> THE BEDROOM

I can hear some of you saying, "That's it? Everybody knows that!" The problem is that many men don't follow what they used to do. Remember how you acted when you were still courting? You should still be doing the same things.

In other words, show your wife that you care about her as a person. Court her all day long:

- Talk to her before going to work.

- Give her as many hugs, pats and kisses during the day as you can.

- Talk to her in the evening. Help her with dinner.

- Ask how her day has gone.

- Praise her for who she is and what she does.

The above list is intended only to spark your own imagination. Add to it; modify it; the important thing is to make sure that what you do comes from your heart. You and your wife need to reestablish your relationship with one another every day. The man who does this will find a different attitude in his wife when they go into the bedroom. He has shown her love throughout the day. She knows that he loves her for who she is.

You see, the actual physical act of making love should be a *natural culmination* of the attitudes created and communicated during that day.

Try it. You and your wife will be pleasantly surprised.

STRENGTHENING EXERCISES

- Men, ask your wife what you could do to be more loving.

- Share with her what you really want to do for her as a husband to make her feel loved and secure.

- Take turns praying for one another.

- Review your "Goals for Becoming a Godly Husband" list.

DAY SIXTEEN

PREPARING THE HEART

Galatians 6:2

2 Carry each other's burdens, and in this way you will fulfill the law of Christ.

Galatians 6:10

10 Therefore, as we have opportunity, let us do good to all people, especially to those who belong to the family of believers.

CHANGING THE HEART

"I can already tell you what will happen when Tom comes home tonight!" Sarah's face is twisted with anger. "He will walk in the door, give me a quick kiss and head straight for the recliner and television. If I try to talk to him about how my day has gone, or what problems I've faced, he will either nod absently or say, 'Not right now.'

"There's <u>never</u> time to really talk." Sarah keeps her eyes on me. Though Tom is sitting next to her, it is as if she will not acknowledge his presence.

"Then he sits down in front of the television for the rest of the evening. Usually, if I'm lucky, he falls asleep. That way I don't have to put up with his wanting to have sex with me."

Tom, of course, sees it differently. "Why should I try to talk with her?" he asks in bewilderment. "All she wants to do is talk about subjects we've already discussed over and over. And she <u>never</u> wants to make love. I can't remember the last time she really responded with any enthusiasm.

"The only thing she does with enthusiasm is nag, nag, nag!"

Here is a marriage with problems. Does it sound like yours? If it does, I have some good news for you. Tom and Sarah were able to put their marriage back on track, with both of them being fulfilled.

Let's see if we can do the same for your marriage. We will begin by working on one area that affects every other area—communication. Be sure to do the strengthening exercises diligently for the next several days.

STRENGTHENING EXERCISES

- Ask your spouse to complete this sentence: "Communication in a marriage means _____."

- Now complete this sentence: "I would feel more like communicating with you if _____."

- Review your "Wish List."

DAY SEVENTEEN

PREPARING THE HEART

Psalm 10:16–18

16 The LORD is King for ever and ever;
   the nations will perish from his land.
17 You hear, O LORD, the desire of the afflicted;
   you encourage them, and you listen to their cry,
18 defending the fatherless and the oppressed,
   in order that man, who is of the earth, may terrify no more.

CHANGING THE HEART

By now you should have realized that several themes run through this book:

- commitment

- self-sacrifice

- communication.

These are the keys to a happy, successful marriage. The three go hand-in-hand into every area of the marital relationship, whether it be financial, sexual, how the housework will be divided, etc.

During the next several days we'll be working on <u>communication</u>. I'll give you two ways to improve this vital area of your relationship.

When a couple in trouble comes to me for counseling, many times you would assume they do not talk to one another. You would be wrong. They not only talk, they complain, they condemn, they accuse and they even scream! But all of this is done *at* one another. It is not communicating.

Perhaps you have fallen into these same habits.

If you want your marriage to improve, take a tip from the Master Communicator. Look carefully at the seventeenth verse of today's devotional. Notice how God communicates with us in three important ways:

- He listens to our cry.

- He hears our desires.

- He encourages us.

If you follow these same three steps with your spouse, communication will be *immediately* introduced into your marriage. You see, the steps are a bridge. They span the chasm of misunderstanding and loneliness. Using this **bridge of communication** helps you move from talking <u>at</u> one another to talking <u>with</u> one another.

The "Strengthening Exercises" will help you construct this powerful bridge in your relationship.

STRENGTHENING EXERCISES

- Ask your spouse to tell you <u>one</u> thing he/she is concerned about.

- Discuss this concern. What can you do to help?

- **Encourage** your spouse by:

    (1) letting him/her know you care;

(2) agreeing to take the responsibility of solving this concern <u>together</u>.

- Take turns praying for your spouse's concerns.

- Review your "Goals for Becoming a Godly Wife" list.

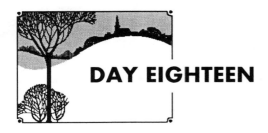

DAY EIGHTEEN

PREPARING THE HEART

Psalms 133

A song of ascents. Of David.

> How good and pleasant it is
> > when brothers live together in unity!
> 2 It is like precious oil poured on the head,
> > running down on the beard,
> running down on Aaron's beard,
> > down upon the collar of his robes.
> 3 It is as if the dew of Hermon
> > were falling on Mount Zion.
> For there the LORD bestows his blessing,
> > even life forevermore.

CHANGING THE HEART

Lloyd Ogilvie tells of the time he was able to reunite a father and son who had not seen each other for twelve years. They had been separated as a result of World War Two. After the two had a chance to talk together for a while, the father exclaimed in joy, "He looks like me, acts like me, and best of all, we think alike. What more can a father ask?"[12]

What indeed? But fathers and sons are not husbands and wives. Let's face it. Even in the best of marriages, most of us don't think like our spouses all the time. When problems occur, we see different solutions. Sometimes we can't even agree on what is a problem. Multiply that out by the number of days in a year, and you begin to see why your marriage might need help.

What is the solution? Learn to communicate.

Think about the last argument you had with your spouse. There might have been talking, but there was probably little communicating being achieved. This is because most of us, when arguing, are more concerned with thinking about what we are going to say than we are with listening to our spouse.

Let's begin changing your arguing habits right now.

Practice saying these two phrases:

- "I understand you are saying....Am I correct?"

- "I understand you feel....Am I correct?"

Here's how you use them.

When your partner says something to you such as, "I hate it because you're never ready on time," the fire begins to rise in your eyes. You launch into an argument about how you never receive any help with getting the children dressed. The argument then goes on from there, with little being accomplished.

Instead, when your spouse complains, you might reply in this way: "I understand you are saying that my not being on time upsets you. Is that correct?"

When you respond like this, at least two things are accomplished:

- You assure your partner that you have heard and understood the complaint.

- You have broken the usual pattern of your marital fighting.

In other words, you have begun **communicating**!

We will look at this technique again tomorrow.

STRENGTHENING EXERCISES

- Read again the first verse in Psalm 133. Do you want that for your marriage?

- Ask your partner to share one complaint with you.

- Respond using one of the two phrases above.

- Continue to talk about the problem *for no more than five minutes*, with each of you using the two key phrases.

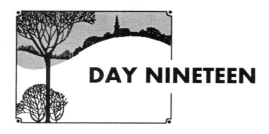

DAY NINETEEN

PREPARING THE HEART

Proverbs 16:20–21, 23–24

20 Whoever gives heed to instruction prospers,
and blessed is he who trusts in the LORD.
21 The wise in heart are called discerning,
and pleasant words promote instruction.
23 A wise man's heart guides his mouth,
and his lips promote instruction.
24 Pleasant words are a honeycomb,
sweet to the soul and healing to the bones.

CHANGING THE HEART

Let's take a moment to talk about yesterday's two key phrases. How did you do using them?

If you're like most of the couples I counsel, at first it seemed awkward. But don't worry. That's only because you are not used to talking like this or interrupting your fighting in this manner. Even though it seems somewhat strange because it's new, **keep on using the phrases.**

Let's look at another example of how this works: "Honey (your spouse might say), it embarrasses me when you joke about me in public."

- Usual response: "You just don't have a sense of humor" or "Quit feeling so thin skinned!"

- New response: "I understand you feel embarrassed when I joke about you in public. Is that correct?"

Now, the next step—the follow-up to one of the key phrases. Go back to the above example. Your spouse has responded, "I understand you feel embarrassed when...." What do you say to that?

You may be tempted to say, "It's about time you finally understand, lunkhead. I've been trying to tell you that for five years!"

Instead, you need to say:

- "Yes. Thank you for understanding."

Or you may need to say:

- "No, that's not exactly what I meant. Let me try to tell you again."

When both of you are absolutely sure the complaint has been correctly stated and understood, the *final step* is ready to be taken.

The person making the complaint then says:

- "What can we do to solve this problem?"

This is another **great solution** to fights and arguments! When you do this, you are initiating true dialogue. Notice how you accomplish this:

- You, the person with the problem, have been given a great gift. Your partner has listened, correctly understood the problem, and has not complained.

- You now give your partner a great gift by telling them you will listen to their solution instead of only offering your own. You have confidence that **together** you can solve the problem.

Your partner will be much more willing to make a change of behavior that he/she helps choose, rather than listening to your advice on how they need to change.

STRENGTHENING EXERCISES

Take turns following these steps:

- (Me) State a problem.

- (You) Use a key phrase. Ask if this is correct.

- (Me) Restate the problem if misunderstood.

- (Me) Once the problem has been correctly understood, thank the other person, then ask spouse to help you find a solution to the problem.

DAY TWENTY

PREPARING THE HEART

Song of Songs 2:15

15 Catch for us the foxes,
　　the little foxes
that ruin the vineyards,
　　our vineyards that are in bloom.

1 John 1:9

9 If we confess our sins, he is faithful and just and will forgive us our sins and purify us from all unrighteousness.

CHANGING THE HEART

Little things, left unsolved, can harm your marriage. The greatest love story in the world knew it, and so should you. These "little foxes" need to be identified and dealt with.

Let me introduce you to one enemy of a good love life which is usually overlooked by many couples. It is dangerous because it seems so normal, so innocent. But this "little fox" is guilty of helping destroy the happiness of countless marriages.

The enemy? **Fatigue.**

Don't laugh. The hectic pace most of us lead exacts a price. While not paid in dollars, the cost is, nevertheless, high. And day in, day out, as you and your spouse subject your bodies to long hours, your enemy grows stronger.

Little by little you find yourself weaker at the end of the day. You only want a good night's sleep. You even promise one another you'll make love "soon."

But soon never seems to come.

There eventually comes a point where you never have enough time or enough energy for much of anything.

And who or what wins the battle of priorities? One author put it like this: "If you don't get enough sleep or sex, sleep will usually take priority!"[13]

The second "little fox" goes along with the first. I call it **Schedule**.

We are busy people. And if we are not careful, our days can become so filled with "important" things that we miss out on one of the most important activities of all—spending time in physical intimacy with our life partner.

If you **schedule** some of these times, you will probably also alter your activities so that **fatigue** doesn't hit you.

Put the "little foxes" out of your marriage immediately!

STRENGTHENING EXERCISES

- Review the list "Our Solutions to Problems."

- Discuss with one another how you can overcome fatigue in your daily life.

- Schedule a time when the two of you can "be together."

DAY TWENTY-ONE

PREPARING THE HEART

Song of Songs 2:2–4

> 2 Like a lily among thorns
>   is my darling among the maidens.
> 3 Like an apple tree among the trees of the forest
>   is my lover among the young men.
> I delight to sit in his shade,
>   and his fruit is sweet to my taste.
> 4 He has taken me to the banquet hall,
>   and his banner over me is love.

CHANGING THE HEART

Remember Tom and Sarah? When we last saw them they were at each other's throats. After that first visit, I had them work on learning how to do two things: **communicate and cuddle**.

- **Communication**—they did some of the same exercises you've been doing in the "Strengthening Exercises" section. After several weeks they were no longer shouting at each other. Instead, they had begun <u>listening</u> when the other talked. This enabled them to solve problems and to begin building trust.

- **Cuddling**—Sarah needed to know that Tom loved her outside the bedroom. Therefore, for one week they did not have sex. Instead, Tom concentrated on giving his wife as many hugs, kisses and pats as she would allow.

Make no mistake, at first it was difficult for both of them to trust the other. **But they did not give up; they kept trying.**

They also learned what sex was and what sex wasn't. Learning that helped them relax in the bedroom. It should also help you.

SEX ISN'T:

- a way to prove your masculinity or femininity,

- a measure of your self-worth,

- a means of resolving marital conflicts,

- another black mark against your mate (if it isn't to your liking),

- <u>just</u> intercourse; it is also cuddling, touching, stroking, sharing warm feelings.[14]

SEX IS:

- a wonderful gift from God,

- a fantastic, sensual, sensory experience,

- a time when the two of you can feel close—as one,

- an experience that improves with practice.

STRENGTHENING EXERCISES

- Share three ways your mate has changed for the better since beginning this book.

- Spend fifteen minutes in bed tonight in each other's arms simply cuddling, talking and laughing.

DAY TWENTY-TWO

PREPARING THE HEART

2 Corinthians 6:11–13

11 We have spoken freely to you, Corinthians, and opened wide our hearts to you. 12 We are not withholding our affection from you, but you are withholding yours from us. 13 As a fair exchange—I speak as to my children—open wide your hearts also.

CHANGING THE HEART

You have something in your possession that can lengthen your life, make you drive safer, and have a healthier body. It's better than health foods, cheaper than having air bags installed in your car, takes no experience to use, and, best of all, <u>costs absolutely nothing</u>!

Too good to be true? Another medical fad? Not at all. This wonder product is (drum roll, please)...

A kiss.

No, don't laugh.

A group of physicians and psychologists, in cooperation with several insurance companies, launched a study to determine what would help married people improve their life. They discovered that if you give your spouse a kiss before going to work, you will miss less work because of illness than those who do not. You will also have

55

fewer auto accidents on the way to work, and live about five years longer. In addition, you will earn 20 to 30 percent more money.

The reason for all these benefits, say the doctors, is simple. Kissers begin the day with a positive attitude.[15]

Take a lesson from the doctors and psychologists. Make a positive impact on your spouse by kissing him/her in the morning before either of you goes to work (it wouldn't hurt to kiss your partner in the afternoon and evening, too!). It will start both of you off with a better attitude.

Or as Paul said, "As a fair exchange...open wide your hearts."

STRENGTHENING EXERCISES

- Take a poll of each other. Ask your spouse how often you kiss him/her during the day.

- Now let's put it another way. How affectionate are you to each other during the day?

- Do both of you think it is enough? If not, start planning to increase the amount beginning tomorrow morning—or even better, start right now!

DAY TWENTY-THREE

PREPARING THE HEART

Galatians 6:7–10

7 Do not be deceived: God cannot be mocked. A man reaps what he sows. 8 The one who sows to please his sinful nature, from that nature will reap destruction; the one who sows to please the Spirit, from the Spirit will reap eternal life. 9 Let us not become weary in doing good, for at the proper time we will reap a harvest if we do not give up. 10 Therefore, as we have opportunity, let us do good to all people, especially to those who belong to the family of believers.

CHANGING THE HEART

Could otters possibly help your marriage?

Gregory Bateson, a renowned anthropologist, was once asked by a zoo to examine their otters. It seems these once active animals were no longer playing with one another. They were listless; they kept to themselves. It actually seemed as if they were depressed!

After observing them for several days, Bateson decided to try an experiment. He took a piece of paper and attached it to a long string. Then he dangled it right over the spot where the otters were resting. In a few moments one otter noticed the paper and began pawing tentatively at it. A second otter joined in, and soon the two were playfully attacking one another. Well, fun is contagious. When the other otters saw what was happening, they had to make sure they weren't left out!

The paper was soon forgotten, but it played its role well. The otters never returned to their listless behavior.

As I said earlier, there is a lesson to be learned from this. Why did Bateson put the paper in with the otters? He knew "as long as nothing new was introduced into the environment, nothing new or different would happen."[16]

Let's be honest. When thinking about the problems in your marriage, you probably envision how your mate needs to change. The problem with this type of thinking is that your mate could be thinking the same thing about you! If each of you keeps waiting for the other to change his/her behavior, <u>nothing will ever improve</u> in your marriage. It's time for *you* to decide to change for the better—no matter what your spouse does. And it will definitely help your marriage.

Remember today's Bible passage:

- You will reap what you sow.

- Don't become weary with doing good.

- Keep on trying! God will bless your efforts.

STRENGTHENING EXERCISES

- Review the two lists "Goals for Becoming a Godly Husband/ Wife."

- What behavior pattern can <u>you</u> change to improve your marriage?

- Pray for the strength to change.

DAY TWENTY-FOUR

PREPARING THE HEART

1 John 2:15–17

15 Do not love the world or anything in the world. If anyone loves the world, the love of the Father is not in him. 16 For everything in the world—the cravings of sinful man, the lust of his eyes and the boasting of what he has and does—comes not from the Father but from the world. 17 The world and its desires pass away, but the man who does the will of God lives forever.

CHANGING THE HEART

It would be easy to become like the farmer who was searching for a mate. He put an ad in the paper that read: "Man 35 wants woman about 25, with tractor. Send picture of tractor."[17]

Selfishness.

Like a cancer, it becomes part of our life if we're not careful. The world proclaims that selfishness is good. The world says it's normal.

The world is wrong.

Examine your life for a moment. Which is more important to you:

• possession of things,

or

- relationships with people.

"Do not love...anything in the world." Why would God say that? Because things break, rust, fall apart.

People last forever.

Put your attention and love upon your life partner, upon your family. You see, loving **things** promotes selfishness and boredom. Loving **people**, especially your spouse, promotes spiritual health and peace.

So...say "no" to the world and "yes" to God.

STRENGTHENING EXERCISES

- Ask your spouse to tell you of any possession that he/she feels you are putting before your marriage.

- If you had to, could you do without that possession?

- What are you willing to do to make your spouse feel at ease about your relationship?

- Review "Our Wish List."

DAY TWENTY-FIVE

PREPARING THE HEART

Matthew 5:1–12

1 Now when he saw the crowds, he went up on a mountainside and sat down. His disciples came to him, 2 and he began to teach them, saying:

3 "Blessed are the poor in spirit,
  for theirs is the kingdom of heaven.
4 Blessed are those who mourn,
  for they will be comforted.
5 Blessed are the meek,
  for they will inherit the earth.
6 Blessed are those who hunger and thirst for righteousness,
  for they will be filled.
7 Blessed are the merciful,
  for they will be shown mercy.
8 Blessed are the pure in heart,
  for they will see God.
9 Blessed are the peacemakers,
  for they will be called sons of God.
10 Blessed are those who are persecuted because of righteousness,
  for theirs is the kingdom of heaven.

11 Blessed are you when people insult you, persecute you and falsely say all kinds of evil against you because of me.

12 Rejoice and be glad, because great is your reward in heaven, for in the same way they persecuted the prophets who were before you."

CHANGING THE HEART

Ready for sacrifice. Ready for service.

The meeting halls of the Quakers were usually barren. They wanted nothing that would distract the eye and heart from worshiping God. But on rare occasions, a lone symbol was allowed. It was an ox placed between a plow and an altar. Beneath it were these words: "Prepared for either."[18]

Ready for sacrifice. Ready for service.

The word "blessed" in the beatitudes can also be translated "happy." Why would God describe the people who inhabit these verses as "happy"? I believe it's because they follow God's principles—no matter what. They are prepared for the one, final act of sacrifice. But they are also prepared for the steady, daily commitment to service.

I don't doubt that most of you would give up your life to save your husband or wife. But are you willing to give up small privileges, on a daily basis, to help your spouse? The Bible has just told us that we will be happy ("blessed") if we adopt these attitudes. So let this be your motto:

Ready for sacrifice. Ready for service.

In other words, follow the path to happiness.

STRENGTHENING EXERCISES

- Are you willing to give your life to save your spouse? Tell him or her of your dedication and love.

- Are you willing to give up other things to help your spouse become happier and more godly? Share this with your partner.

- Review the exercises on pages 43–44.

DAY TWENTY-SIX

PREPARING THE HEART

Matthew 18:21–35

21 Then Peter came to Jesus and asked, "Lord, how many times shall I forgive my brother when he sins against me? Up to seven times?"

22 Jesus answered, "I tell you, not seven times, but seventy-seven times.

23 "Therefore, the kingdom of heaven is like a king who wanted to settle accounts with his servants. 24 As he began the settlement, a man who owed him ten thousand talents was brought to him. 25 Since he was not able to pay, the master ordered that he and his wife and his children and all that he had be sold to repay the debt.

26 "The servant fell on his knees before him. 'Be patient with me,' he begged, 'and I will pay back everything.' 27 The servant's master took pity on him, canceled the debt and let him go.

28 "But when that servant went out, he found one of his fellow servants who owed him a hundred denarii. He grabbed him and began to choke him. 'Pay back what you owe me!' he demanded.

29 "His fellow servant fell to his knees and begged him, 'Be patient with me, and I will pay you back.'

30 "But he refused. Instead, he went off and had the man thrown into prison until he could pay the debt. 31 When the other servants saw what had happened, they were greatly distressed and went and told their master everything that had happened.

32 "Then the master called the servant in. 'You wicked servant,' he said, 'I canceled all that debt of yours because you begged me to. 33 Shouldn't you have had mercy on your fellow servant just as I had on you?' 34 In anger his master turned him over to the jailers to be tortured, until he should pay back all he owed.

35 "This is how my heavenly Father will treat each of you unless you forgive your brother from your heart."

CHANGING THE HEART

"The Mission" is a film about forgiveness. It shows us the life of a slave trader in the 18th century. Not content with robbing South American villages of their children, he also robs his own family. At one point, in a fit of jealousy, he kills his younger brother.

This selfish, angry man eventually has a change of heart and gives his life to God. But try as he might, he cannot rid himself of the horror of his crimes. Finally he determines to go back to South America, back to one of the villages he has raided and ask forgiveness—and perhaps lose his life in the process.

Upon reaching the continent, he decides that even greater sacrifice is called for. So this haunted man embarks upon an unusual act of penance. Everything used in his former profession—armor, breastplate, helmet and swords—he now ties around his neck. As he makes his way through the jungle, his burdens weigh heavy upon him, hindering his progress. They also make a deafening noise.

The villagers can hear him coming from far away. They know who he is. They know why he has come. And they make their preparations.

After many days the former slave trader finally stumbles into the village. He is exhausted, nearly dead from the effort of dragging through the jungle the objects representing his former life. The worst thought for him, however, is this: his act of penance has brought him no peace.

Looking up, he sees the entire village assembled. One of the men, a warrior, takes a sword and rushes at him. The blade swoops at his neck. Death is imminent. Then, in amazement, he sees instead the sword bite through the rope holding the armor and weapons. They go clanging down the side of the mountain.

Amid tears of joy, the man realizes he is forgiven. No longer must he carry the weight of yesterday around his tired body and soul.[19]

Are you carrying around burdens God never intended you to have? Ask forgiveness for your past wrongs. Let them go. Give them to God.

And one more thing. Read verse 35 again. This applies to you and your relationship with your spouse.

Have you forgiven him/her of things done to you in the past? Or are you hugging them to you, constantly thinking of them, allowing them to wound you repeatedly? If you want true freedom and happiness, forgive your partner.

Do it now.

STRENGTHENING EXERCISES

- Is there something for which you have still not forgiven your spouse? Give it to God now.

- Ask your spouse if there is something he or she feels you are still holding against them.

- Be sure to pray. Ask God to give you a spirit of forgiveness.

DAY TWENTY-SEVEN

PREPARING THE HEART

2 Timothy 2:14–16

14 Keep reminding them of these things. Warn them before God against quarreling about words; it is of no value, and only ruins those who listen. 15 Do your best to present yourself to God as one approved, a workman who does not need to be ashamed and who correctly handles the word of truth. 16 Avoid godless chatter, because those who indulge in it will become more and more ungodly.

CHANGING THE HEART

"I don't think I should have to...." Can you finish the phrase? But be careful; those words are dangerous! They contribute to trouble in countless marriages.

"I don't think I should have to...

- ...tell my husband to help with the housework."

- ...tell my wife how I'm going to spend my Saturdays."

- ...give up one day a week to visit my spouse's parents."

The list goes on and on. Listen to what Michele Weiner-Davis has to say about this phrase.

Sometimes when I ask a person what seems to work I hear, "I know my wife is more understanding about my absences when I call her every day when I'm on a business trip, but <u>I don't think I should have to do that</u>. She should just trust me." Or "My husband puts the kids to bed when I ask him to, but he should just think of it himself." She should and he should, but they don't! So don't sit back waiting for your mate to change when you already have the formula for success.[20]

The phrase "I don't think I should have to...." solves nothing and hinders much in your marriage. Decide right now that you and your spouse will work on eliminating that phrase from your marriage.

Replace it with a new phrase: **"I DON'T HAVE TO LIKE IT, I JUST HAVE TO DO IT!"**[21]

In other words, if it helps your marriage, go on and give a little. And you never can tell. You just might learn to like it!

STRENGTHENING EXERCISES

- Think of 2 things you don't think you ought to have to do—but that you **will** do to help the marriage.

- Write them down on the next page under "Things I don't <u>have</u> to do, but I <u>will</u> do."

- Review the list "Our Solutions to Problems."

- Will doing these four things help solve the problems on that list?

THINGS I DON'T HAVE TO DO, BUT I WILL DO

Husband:

_____

_____

_____

_____

_____

_____

_____

_____

_____

_____

_____

_____

_____

_____

_____

_____

Wife:

_____

_____

_____

_____

_____

_____

_____

_____

_____

_____

_____

_____

_____

_____

_____

_____

_____

DAY TWENTY-EIGHT

PREPARING THE HEART

Psalms 103:8–12

> 8 The LORD is compassionate and gracious,
>   slow to anger, abounding in love.
> 9 He will not always accuse,
>   nor will he harbor his anger forever;
> 10 he does not treat us as our sins deserve
>   or repay us according to our iniquities.
> 11 For as high as the heavens are above the earth,
>   so great is his love for those who fear him;
> 12 as far as the east is from the west,
>   so far has he removed our transgressions from us.

Hebrews 8:12

> 12 For I will forgive their wickedness
>   and will remember their sins no more.

CHANGING THE HEART

Let me ask you two questions.

When you and your spouse argue, how much of the time is spent bringing up and talking about the past? When you think negative thoughts about your spouse, how much of those thoughts have to do with past events you have played out over and over in your mind?

Now let me give you a fact.

You cannot defend yourself against the past. Because no matter how many times you bring it up, the past cannot be changed.

One more question, please.

If the past cannot be changed, why do you cling to it so much in your arguments? Aren't you glad God doesn't cling to <u>your</u> past, refusing to let go of it and forgive you!

Let go of the past. Resolve not to bring it up in future arguments. Letting go will shorten your arguments and lengthen your tempers!

Here is a good phrase to remember when you're tempted to use the past as a weapon:

- **"That was then. This is now. We can all change."**

Letting go of the past means you can get on with your life. It frees your marriage of negative thinking and allows the two of you to concentrate on what <u>can be</u> instead of on what <u>was</u>.

STRENGTHENING EXERCISES

- What events in the past do you need to let go of?

- Agree to use the above phrase the next time one of you is guilty of using the past during an argument.

- Thank God for forgiving you of your wrongs. Now forgive one another.

DAY TWENTY-NINE

PREPARING THE HEART

Luke 15:11–23

11 Jesus continued: "There was a man who had two sons.

12 The younger one said to his father, 'Father, give me my share of the estate.' So he divided his property between them.

13 "Not long after that, the younger son got together all he had, set off for a distant country and there squandered his wealth in wild living. 14 After he had spent everything, there was a severe famine in that whole country, and he began to be in need. 15 So he went and hired himself out to a citizen of that country, who sent him to his fields to feed pigs. 16 He longed to fill his stomach with the pods that the pigs were eating, but no one gave him anything.

17 "When he came to his senses, he said, 'How many of my father's hired men have food to spare, and here I am starving to death! 18 I will set out and go back to my father and say to him: Father, I have sinned against heaven and against you. 19 I am no longer worthy to be called your son; make me like one of your hired men.' 20 So he got up and went to his father.

"But while he was still a long way off, his father saw him and was filled with compassion for him; he ran to his son, threw his arms around him and kissed him.

21 "The son said to him, 'Father, I have sinned against heaven and against you. I am no longer worthy to be called your son.'

22 "But the father said to his servants, 'Quick! Bring the best robe and put it on him. Put a ring on his finger and sandals on his feet. 23 Bring the fattened calf and kill it. Let's have a feast and celebrate.'"

CHANGING THE HEART

The two children were far from home. Despite repeated warnings, they had followed a small rabbit into the great forest near where they lived. Now, as the sun began to set and the shadows lengthened menacingly, they realized the seriousness of what they had done.

There is nothing like the blackness of night in a thick wood. The children shivered and looked around desperately, trying to see a familiar landmark. Suddenly, the oldest became panicked. "Help!" he shouted. "We're lost! Please help!"

To their surprise, a voice responded, "Stay where you are. I'll be there in a minute."

Sure enough, the two children soon saw a light moving in the distance. Someone had come searching for them. When they realized who it was, they gave a glad cry. Jumping into their father's arms, they snuggled close to this strong man who loved them.

The darkness was forgotten. Their father had found his precious children.

This story is for you.

You and your spouse are the children. The father is God, your Heavenly Father. Perhaps you have wandered away from Him, following people or things that initially seemed attractive. Now you realize you are lost.

Do as the children did. Call out to God. Acknowledge your wrongs, ask forgiveness and let Jesus Christ cleanse you from all your past indiscretions. The greatest gift you can give to one another as husband and wife is to have a change of heart by submitting to the love of God.

God is looking for you. He is waiting. He wants to live with you forever.

STRENGTHENING EXERCISES

- If you are unsure of your relationship to God, I encourage you to pray aloud the following prayer.

- "Dear God, I know I've done some things that are wrong and I'm sorry for my sins. I believe your son Jesus Christ died on the cross to pay the penalty for my sins.

  "Right now, in the best way I know how, I open my life to you. Please come into my life and forgive me of my sins. Make me clean and pure, live with me forever, and take me to heaven when I die.

  "Thank you for coming into my life. Thank you for making me a Christian. Now help me to live for you daily. In Jesus' Name, Amen."

- Find a good, Bible-believing church and begin attending regularly.

DAY THIRTY

PREPARING THE HEART

1 Corinthians 13:4–8a

4 Love is patient, love is kind. It does not envy, it does not boast, it is not proud. 5 It is not rude, it is not self-seeking, it is not easily angered, it keeps no record of wrongs. 6 Love does not delight in evil but rejoices with the truth. 7 It always protects, always trusts, always hopes, always perseveres.

8 Love never fails.

CHANGING THE HEART

"Where do we go from here?"

It's a question you might be asking yourselves. After all, this is the last day of the book.

If both of you have been faithful in reading the devotionals and working on the "Strengthening Exercises," then you've covered a lot of ground. And you have probably seen some improvement.

So, a suggestion.

Why not continue meeting for fifteen minutes every day? By this time, you know the value of time spent together talking and sharing.

"Where do we go from here?"

Don't forget the exercises on page 47. Continue to refer to them often as an aid to your communication. Review your lists at least once a month, in order to see how you're progressing.

"Where do we go from here?"

Charles Dickens, the great British author, was taking a walk in London one beautiful afternoon. Two women watched him carefully, for his head was constantly turning in different directions. A bus passing by would catch his attention, then perhaps a bird overhead, or a child playing in the park. He seemed delighted and overwhelmed by the experience of life.

"Excuse me, sir," one of the ladies finally ventured. "Where are you going?"

"Going? Going?" Dickens replied, his eyes shining with enthusiasm. "Why, ladies, I'm going **forward**!"

"Where do we go from here?"

Follow the example of Dickens. Put the past behind you and go forward—together!

STRENGTHENING EXERCISES

- The scripture passage you read today is the same one which began this book. How have you changed between the first day and this one?

- Review all your lists.

- Decide to continue spending fifteen minutes each day talking, praying and sharing together with your spouse.

- Take a moment to pray. Thank God for your marriage. Ask Him to continue strengthening it.

CONCLUSION

Let me give you one more thing before we close. I call it the

FORMULA FOR SUCCESS.

Believe me, it can help your marriage have a bright future.

Let's begin with what you *don't* put in! Be sure to leave **THE BIG MISTAKE** out of your marriage. It's ironic, but even though **THE BIG MISTAKE** can create a huge hole in your relationship, it is hard to spot. In fact many marriages, in trying to make progress over the years, repeat this mistake over and over—and never realize it!

What is **THE BIG MISTAKE?**

It's a thought process that goes something like this: *We've done well this past month. We're communicating better than ever. Our disagreements are fewer; our love is deeper.* <u>*So we can probably stop the devotionals and the fifteen minutes talking with each other every day.*</u>

WRONG!

Remember this: your marriage has changed for the better *because your habits have changed.* If you go back to the old way of living your life and relating to each other, your marriage will probably slip back to the old, cold way, as well.

• So, the first ingredient is: Avoid **THE BIG MISTAKE**.

Keep reading the Bible together, talking together and praying to God together.

- The second ingredient: **Commitment.**

Right now, stop and commit to each other that you will continue doing this *every day*. If one of you has to be away from home, use the telephone to have a "long distance" Bible reading and prayer with each other. (A tip: one way to help ensure time for the devotional is to **commit** time to Bible reading and prayer *before* spending time watching television!)

Before we leave **Commitment**, let's honor God by doing something right now. Take your spouse—your "life-partner"—by the hand and together, offer up this prayer to God: *Heavenly Father, we commit our marriage to you. We pledge to make spending time together with you a daily priority. Please take control of our lives, take control of this relationship, and take control of our family. Help each of us to be the husband and wife we should be. As we read the Bible together and pray every day, may you be the Lord of this marriage. In Jesus' Name we ask these things. Amen.*

- The third ingredient: **Review.**

Find a calendar. Circle one day a month for the next six months. On that day, go back over the lists you filled out on pages 10, 13, 16, 20, 68, and 69 in this book.

- The fourth ingredient: **Devotional Helps.**

If you're looking for more sources to help you with devotionals, you might want to go to your local bookstore and check out the following:

(1) *NIV Couples Devotional Bible*, Zondervan Publishing House (365 devotionals for couples).

(2) *Moments Together for Couples*, by Dennis and Barbara Rainey, Regal Books (a year's worth of devotionals).

(3) *Fifteen Minute Devotions for Couples*, by Bob & Emily Barnes, Harvest House.

(4) *Family Walk*, by Walk Through the Bible Ministries, Zondervan.

(5) *Quiet Times for Couples*, by H. Norman Wright, Harvest House Publishers.

(6) *God's Little Devotional Book for Couples*, Honor Books.

Now you know the formula. Together, grow in your love for each other, and in your love for God.

If this book has made a significant difference in your marriage, I'd like to know about it. You can write me at: Mark Sutton/ 8900 Kingston Rd./ Shreveport, LA 71118. Or you can E-mail me at Mark_Sutton@msn.com.

NOTES

1. James Dobson, *Love For A Lifetime* (Portland, Oreg.: Multnomah Press, 1987), pg. 42.
2. Ibid.
3. *HOMEMADE* Newsletter, Family Concern (Morrison, Colo.)
4. *Curious Customs*, Tad Tuleja (New York: Harmony Books, 1987), pgs. 59–60.
5. "There is neither Jew nor Greek, slave nor free, male nor female, for you are all one in Christ Jesus." (Galatians 3:28)
6. *Homiletics*, April–June 1991 (Canton, Ohio: Communication Resources), pg. 18.
7. *Bits and Pieces*, Nov. 14, 1991 (Fairfield, N.J.), pgs. 2–3.
8. *Christianity Today*, Jan. 14, 1991 (Coral Stream, Ill.), pg. 40.
9. David McKechnie, *Experiencing God's Pleasure* (Nashville: Oliver Nelson, 1989), pg. 125.
10. *Leadership*, Oct. 29, 1991 (Fairfield, N.J.: The Economics Press, Inc.), pg. 16.
11. William J. Bausch, *Storytelling—Imagination and Faith* (Mystic, Conn.: Twenty-third Publishers, 1989), pg. 67.
12. Lloyd Ogilvie, *The Other Jesus* (Waco, Tex.: Word Books, 1986), pg. 196.
13. Janet L. Wolfe, *What to Do When He Has a Headache* (New York: Hyperion, 1992), pg. 7.
14. Ibid., pg. 87.
15. "Bits and Pieces," July 25, 1992 (Fairfield, N.J.: The Economics Press, Inc.), pgs. 4–5.
16. Michele Weiner-Davis, *Divorce Busting* (New York: Summit Books, 1992), pg. 146.
17. *Our Daily Bread*, May 1992.
18. "Homiletics", July–September 1991 (Canton, Ohio: Communication Resources), pgs. 33–34.
19. Jay Strack, from a sermon given at the Southern Baptist Convention's Pastors' Conference, Indianapolis, Indiana, June 8, 1992.
20. Michele Weiner-Davis, *Divorce Busting* (New York: Summit Books, 1992), pg. 132.
21. Ibid.